GAWAIN

A Libretto

GAWAIN

David Harsent

Universal Edition

First published in Great Britain in 1991
by Universal Edition (London) Limited, London.

Copyright © 1991 Universal Edition (London) Limited, London

The right of David Harsent to be identified as author of this
work has been asserted by him in accordance with the
Copyright, Designs and Patents Act 1988

ISBN 0 900938 70 6
UE 26933L

Typesetting by Ternary Graphics, Hither Green, London
Cover design by Dewynters Plc
Reproduced and Printed in Great Britain by
Halstan & Co. Ltd., Amersham, Bucks., England

to Simon

Preface

In making this version of *Sir Gawain and the Green Knight* for music theatre I have retained little of the original save the essential narrative drift. It was clear from the outset that the Gawain poet's language and metre, however loosely rendered, were going to be of limited use to me in composing parts to be sung on a modern stage. From time to time, I have made use of moments of direct speech, though these are often displaced, added to, or bent to my story's purpose; and a number of descriptive passages have been reworked as dialogue. Of course, there are some lines in the poem that offer an opportunity for something akin to a translation: moments at Castle Hautdesert, for example, or passages where the Green Knight and others are given speech that promotes narrative progression. For the most part, though, the poem doesn't provide much for a dramatic version and I was glad to be freed into my own composition and, so far as the investigation of character and motive go, my own discoveries and inventions.

One or two practical changes were necessary. In the poem, Bertilak's wife is never named. For the sake of convenience, I have called her Lady de Hautdesert, thereby ennobling her husband – reasonably enough, it seemed to me. I have also introduced her with Morgan at the beginning of the piece, in a role that clearly identifies her as Morgan's accomplice – a structural change that meets what seemed a dramatic necessity when the fact of the sung line makes it advisable to be more than usually clear about character, motive and plot.

This libretto existed in several drafts. The first few versions involved the usual business of successive revisions. During that time, I didn't give much thought to the music or the staging.

I was conscious, of course, that my words had to be singable and my narrative comprehensible; and I was typically profligate with stage directions. However, I completed my verse play without taking account of whatever needs the music might eventually develop. The final draft had precisely to do with those needs. The changes the libretto took then were the result of pressure of composition from another source.

To begin with, Harrison Birtwistle and I hadn't felt the need to do much more than agree a subject and, in effect, agree to trust one another. As the score progressed, our collaboration grew richer and more complex. Any writing intended for the stage will find or lose chances as other opinions, other ways of seeing, affect it – a director's, an actor's, perhaps the writer's own altered view of things when the play comes to rehearsal. We were eager for such chances; but the four-year conversation between Harry and myself was a much more intense affair than that. This was not an example of interpretive arts taking up a text that, when a certain production, a certain concert, is over, will remain the same, but a process where one vision was bound to find a way of accommodating the needs of another.

Sometimes I made changes because of what the music was doing in composition. For example, the 'Turning of the Seasons' passage found its proper textual length, shape and density as the music of that section was approached, reached, and then composed. The poet gave it thirty-six lines. In my first draft, Morgan and Bertilak's wife shared ten quatrains. Second thoughts combined those stanzas with a description of the arming of Gawain for his journey, as if the beginning and the end of that event could take us from winter to winter. Eventually, it became the long, central, transitional passage that closes the first act and demonstrates more clearly than anything else the circular and ritual aspects of the opera.

At other times, a rewrite would seem to have more to do

with considerations of stagecraft (Gawain's return to the court was such a moment); often, though, these demands were revealed to be the same thing – what the music was doing dictated the changes we were making to what would (saving a director's contribution) happen on stage. Invariably, it was a case of additional text.

Throughout, our collaboration was in support of the piece and in support of each other. I suspect that we'd both been prepared to wage war if need be. It was clear, pretty much from the outset, that it wasn't going to be necessary. Our separate visions of the opera (or of what it might become) were sufficiently sympathetic to prevent a quick breakdown of ideas; the ways in which they differed made us curious. We started from there.

D.H.
March 1991

GAWAIN

an opera

Words by David Harsent

Set to music by Harrison Birtwistle

Dramatis Personae

Morgan le Fay	Arthur's half-sister; Gawain's aunt
Lady de Hautdesert	Wife of Bertilak
Arthur	King of Logres
Guinevere	Arthur's wife
A Fool	
Agravain	A knight; Gawain's brother; Arthur's nephew by his half-sister Belisent
Ywain	A knight; Arthur's nephew by his half-sister Brimesent
Gawain	A knight; Arthur's nephew by his half-sister Belisent; brother of Agravain.
Bishop Baldwin	Arthur's confessor and spiritual guide
The Green Knight Bertilak de Hautdesert	]

Production note

It ought to be mentioned that the Green Chapel is not a building. The Gawain poet describes it thus:

> A bawle berwe by a bonk the brymme biside...

> Hit had a hole on the ende and on ayther side,
> And overgrowen with gres in glodes aywhere,
> And all was holw unwith, nobot an olde cave
> Or a crevisse of an olde cragge...

> (A smooth-surfaced barrow beside a stream...

> It had a hole at one end and at either side,
> And was overgrown with grass in great clumps;
> It was hollow, nothing more than an old cave
> Or a fissure in some ancient crag...)

GAWAIN was commissioned by the Royal Opera House, Covent Garden and first performed there in May 1991.

Act One

Arthur's court. On stage: Guinevere, Agravian, Ywain, Gawain, Baldwin, The Fool *and* Arthur. *Also on stage, but unseen by the others:* Morgan le Fay *and* Lady de Hautdesert.

MORGAN

Night after night, the same dream –
to be in this place,
unseen, untouchable, my breath
dousing their faces...

Arthur and Guinevere
foxed by passion and fame,
at ease with their youth
as if they could live for ever, as if
nothing could tarnish or grow old.

Now, at the year's dead end,
the dream quickens – my enemies
under my hand,
the old wounds opening.

LADY DE HAUTDESERT

Morgan! Your purpose chills me
and excites me: blood feud,

14

blood pact, the bonds
of treachery and kinship.

Day after day, the same promise –
a figure crossing a landscape,
travelling towards me...
A face I could almost see,
a meeting already rehearsed.

Someone here will become inescapable,
climbing into focus
minute by minute, footstep by footstep,
a distant voice, a name I could almost utter.

The promise is renewed
now, at the year's dead end.

MORGAN, LADY DE HAUTDESERT

The season deepens,
the moor
is battened under ice;
the world is a single colour,
the wind its only voice.

The day darkens;
in hall
firelight sweats the stone.
Now celebrate the hearth,
the boar's head and the wine.

Winter's crop
is death,
seed in the frozen stone,
the forest's iron rafters,
the scorch of frost on fern.

At Christmas-tide
all sing
the Child unborn and dance
hand over hand: the warp
and weft of innocence.

The world outside
confides
an image from a dream –
low over the snowfield
the crow's black cruciform.

The world indoors
confirms
a pact, this holy day,
with fealty, laughter, love,
courage, humility.

ARTHUR

    ...they tire me –
rituals of the season tamed by habit,
niggardly movement, insipid, formal smiles.
Men should have nobler causes, nobler fears.

GUINEVERE

Arthur – join us.
Come and eat.

ARTHUR

Who's brave?
Who'll prove his courage to me?
Who'll spice my food
with news of foreign wars,

of battle-shouts and colours
brought home in glory?

Arthur...come and eat.

ARTHUR

Some fable of bravery, then.
Some traveller's tale
to make me mad, to bleed into my sleep.
I've heard
of toads with woman's breasts, of birds with fangs...
Pagan things... The hare
who sleeps with open eyes, or throws herself
into a fire and stares back from the blaze
unmarked, unharmed...
The castor, who emasculates himself;
the griffin, lion-haunched and eagle masked;
the unicorn
trapped in a virgin's lap.
Men have seen such things.
The yena, sometimes female, sometimes male,
who chants in a human voice
and lives in graveyards, feeding off the dead.
Men have seen them.

We see the figure of a knight travelling through a landscape.

GUINEVERE

Come and sit by me.

ARTHUR

Who's brave?

17

who'll make the journey
over the badlands of sleep,
trekking through clods and brine,
through mists and swarming shadows,
to meet himself there
waiting for the worst dream to begin?

MORGAN, LADY DE HAUTDESERT

Soon you'll see its face,
soon you'll hear its voice.

ARTHUR

Who's brave?
Tell me my bloodline.

THE FOOL

There was a man
whose strength
grew with the rising sun...
Who is it?

AGRAVAIN

Cuchulain...

THE FOOL

There was a man
born to an island king
and named the Hawk of May...
Who is it?

YWAIN

Gwalchmai...

THE FOOL

There was a man
conceived by sorcery...
Who –

GAWAIN

Pendragon's son – Arthur.

ARTHUR

How can I eat?
Can't someone whet
my appetite with courage?
Anyone...show me a test.

THE FOOL

There was a man...

MORGAN, LADY DE HAUTDESERT

Soon. What you most love
and what you fear...

Soon. What you want you'll have;
it's almost here...

ARTHUR

Tell me my bloodline:
how one man challenged seven,
how another was witched
by four queens. Tell what happened
aboard the miraculous ship; and tell
the vision of the raven and the swan.
Tell me –

THE FOOL

There was a man –

MORGAN, LADY DE HAUTDESERT

Soon you'll see its face.

THE FOOL

– who fell from grace...

GUINEVERE

Come and take your place.

MORGAN, LADY DE HAUTDESERT

What you want you'll have;
what you love and fear.

Morgan *and* Lady de Hautdesert *dance.*

THE FOOL

There was a man
who fell from grace...
Who is it?

We hear a knock at the door.

MORGAN, LADY DE HAUTDESERT

This is the hour of legacy or loss.
This is the hour of vanity or choice.

We hear a knock at the door. It begins to open.

LADY DE HAUTDESERT

Soon you'll see its face.

MORGAN

Soon you'll hear its voice.

The door is fully open. It begins to close again.

ARTHUR

It's nothing...nothing...nothing...
a game, an escapade,
Christmas mummery, a raree show...

GUINEVERE

Come and take your place.

MORGAN, LADY DE HAUTDESERT

This is the moment that waited for you
as you journeyed towards it.
This is the moment you carried with you
from the worst dream.

THE FOOL

Something stranger than charity,
something greener than grief,
something colder than justice,
more secret, more stern than belief.

What is it?

We hear a knock at the door.

MORGAN, LADY DE HAUTDESERT

Now is the hour of legacy or loss.

We hear a knock at the door.

MORGAN, LADY DE HAUTDESERT

Now is the hour of vanity or choice.

We hear a knock at the door. It begins to open.

LADY DE HAUTDESERT

Now you'll see its face

MORGAN

Now you'll hear its voice.

The door is open. We see The Green Knight.

MORGAN

Now I shall test his strength with mine,
his purpose with mine, his appetite with mine –

LADY DE HAUTDESERT

as kinship is tested by grief,

MORGAN

as hatred is tested by time,

LADY DE HAUTDESERT

as honour is tested by pity,

MORGAN

as truth is tested by fear,

LADY DE HAUTDESERT

as virtue is tested by need,

MORGAN

as courage is tested by reason.

The Green Knight *enters, on horseback.*

THE GREEN KNIGHT

Which of you is king?

BALDWIN,

God's name!

YWAIN

You dare!

GAWAIN

A test!

AGRAVAIN

A hoax!

ARTHUR

Welcome...welcome...welcome...welcome...
Do you want food? – There's food;
the wine has been blessed.

BALDWIN

God's name...
Eripe me
Domine, ad homine male...

ARTHUR

Will you sit with us?

23

Here's your place.

THE GREEN KNIGHT

I'm told there are brave men here...

ARTHUR

Ah... Then choose your ground
and choose your man.
No one will flinch from it.

BALDWIN,

God's name!

YWAIN

You dare...

GAWAIN

Choose me.

AGRAVAIN

Choose...

ARTHUR

Choose, choose, choose.

THE GREEN KNIGHT

Choose? From these beardless boys?
I haven't come to fight –
did you think that?
This token of peace,
these soft clothes...
Who could have stood against me

24

in my armour?

                 No –
I bring a gift –
it's Christmas-tide.

MORGAN

Now he knows its face...

BALDWIN

Witchcraft...

GAWAIN

A hoax...

THE GREEN KNIGHT

A test; a game...
Who's brave?
Are you, Arthur?

BALDWIN, YWAIN, GAWAIN, AGRAVAIN

You dare...

LADY DE HAUTDESERT

Now he hears its voice.

THE GREEN KNIGHT

Here is the challenge – one of you
must swing the axe at me.
I must bow my head
and bare my neck to take the cutting-edge.
I must not turn aside or duck the blow.

ARTHUR

And then?

THE GREEN KNIGHT

Then he must stand
and take the same from me.

ARTHUR

A man strikes you – ?

THE GREEN KNIGHT

I must not turn aside
or duck the blow –

ARTHUR

(Indicates his neck)

Here – ?

THE GREEN KNIGHT

With this –
then takes the same from me.
He must not turn aside
or duck the blow.

BALDWIN

Witchcraft. The Devil's here.

ARTHUR

How will you kill a man
if you are dead?
When will your opponent pay his debt?

26

THE GREEN KNIGHT

In one year and a day –
that's his reprieve;
my turn comes then.

Who'll do it? Who's brave.

BALDWIN

Custodi me, Domine,
de manu peccatoris:
et ab hominibus
iniquis eripe me.

THE GREEN KNIGHT

Is this Arthur's house?
Do you talk of victories,
of battles, of reckless ventures,
of trophies taken against piling odds?

Is this the place?

Do you talk of such things?
Do you remember them?
What if your fathers
witnessed this; your father's fathers?
Tell me your bloodline.

I came here looking for a man
whose courage shone from his face.
I thought he would be the man legend forgot,

no fireside hero, no armchair warrior
fierce with words, reminding everyone
how he became the pivot of the plot,

27

his name on every lip, his voice
belling the battlefield...
I know those songs; I know they make you hot;

they leave me cold. I came to find a man
whose courage shone from his face.
He isn't here. There's a smell
of timidity in the place, like rot.

MORGAN

This is the hour of vanity or choice.

LADY DE HAUTDESERT

This is the hour of legacy or loss.

BALDWIN

God's name...

ARTHUR

Give me the axe.

YWAIN

You dare...

AGRAVAIN

You dare...

GAWAIN

I'll do it – hoax or test;
release me from my place

Tell me your name.

GAWAIN

Gawain.

THE GREEN KNIGHT

     Gawain... You make
your choice my choice. Now we shall come
to know each other. Now we shall grow
more like each other. As your hand grasps the axe –
feel my hand there; and when you see my head
lopped and fallen, my eyes clouded with blood,
my mouth awash with blood –
see both our faces there: my eyes, your eyes;
my mouth, your mouth; my blood, your blood.

GAWAIN

What I shall see is what will happen next –
your body polled and pruned, like any tree
cut back to give more light.
My hand on the axe, and your head fallen.
Your eyes, your mouth, your blood.

THE GREEN KNIGHT

You understand the pact?

GAWAIN

In twelve months and a day
I'll stand a blow from you. The first cut's mine.

BALDWIN

Witchcraft!

THE GREEN KNIGHT

You think I won't survive...
But if I live
I'll tell you where to find me;
if I don't
then stay at home and lead a quiet life
and prosper with the women and the dogs.

BALDWIN

Domine convertere
et eripe animam meam:
salvum me fac propter
misericordiam tuam.

GAWAIN

The terms are yours.

THE GREEN KNIGHT

They are.

GAWAIN

The first cut's mine –
the first, also the last.
When your head's off
and rolling on the floor,
tell me then
how to take my turn;
tell me then
how I shall find you

in twelve months and a day;
and tell me then
who prospers, and who is God's.

Gawain *begins to raise the axe. We see the figure of a knight travelling through the landscape of 'the world outdoors'.*

MORGAN, LADY DE HAUTDESERT

This is the moment that waited for you
as you journeyed towards it.

This is the moment you carried with you
from the worst dream.

THE FOOL

Something bolder than vanity,
something darker than shame,
something swifter than pity,
more zealous, more lavish, than fame.

What is it?

We hear a knock at the door

MORGAN, LADY DE HAUTDESERT

Now is the hour of legacy or loss.

We hear a knock at the door.

MORGAN, LADY DE HAUTDESERT

Now is the hour of vanity or choice.

The door begins to open.

Now you'll see its face.

MORGAN

Now you'll hear its voice.

The door is open. We see The Green Knight, *who enters and bows his head. As before, we see the figure of a knight, travelling through the landscape.* Gawain *raises the axe.* Morgan *and* Lady de Hautdesert *dance.* Gawain *strikes the blow, decapitating* The Green Knight *and covering himself and* Guinevere *in blood.*

GUINEVERE, BALDWIN, ARTHUR, YWAIN, FOOL, AGRAVAIN

God's name!

THE GREEN KNIGHT

Gawain...

MORGAN, LADY DE HAUTDESERT

Now you hear its voice.
Now you see its face.

GUINEVERE, BALDWIN, ARTHUR, YWAIN, FOOL, AGRAVAIN

God's name!

The Green Knight *lifts his severed head and sings.*

THE GREEN KNIGHT

My title
is Knight of the Green Chapel –
in one year and a day
look for me there...a place
more like hill than a house,

more like a cave than a hill,
more like a tomb than a cave.

Ride north: you'll hear my name
spoken by those you meet. Ride north:
full-face to the ice-wind
over the winter badlands.
Your dreams of death
from this day to that day
will journey with you
from this place to that place –
like something you've hoarded,
like something you need to own...

Woodland creatures,
your image trapped in their eyes;
creatures of the night, taking your scent;
madmen who know
only one word – your name.

Ride north.
Find the place and find me there.
The bargain's struck. You carry it
closer than your shadow.

Find the place. Ride north. Until that time
remember your dreams...
Think only of dreams and promises.

GAWAIN

In twelve months and a day
I'll stand a blow from you...

The Green Knight *mounts his horse.*

THE GREEN KNIGHT

Ride north...find me there...

GAWAIN

In twelve months and a day...

The door begins to open. The Green Knight *rides through.*

ARTHUR

It's nothing...nothing...nothing...
a game...an escapade...
Christmas mummery...a raree show...

THE GREEN KNIGHT

(Off)

Ride north...ride north...
find the place...

ARTHUR

Look: I've seen something
to wonder at. Now I can eat.
Hang up the axe; the moment's gone.
Up there –
where everyone can see it and remember.

GUINEVERE

This is the hour of vanity and choice.

As before, we see the figure of a knight travelling through the landscape of 'the world outdoors'.

MORGAN, LADY DE HAUTDESERT

The contract can't be broken;

LADY DE HAUTDESERT

it's your burden.

MORGAN

You've given your word on this;

MORGAN, LADY DE HAUTDESERT

you're Arthur's token.

GUINEVERE

This is the hour of legacy and loss.

MORGAN, LADY DE HAUTDESERT

Now that you've seen its face,
now that you've made your choice;
now that you've heard its voice,
now that you know its price...

ARTHUR

It was an act –
a Christmas sideshow.

MORGAN, LADY DE HAUTDESERT

This is your pact,
you carry it
closer than your shadow.

*There follows the 'Turning of the Seasons' section, during which
Gawain is stripped, washed and armed. During each of the following
five sections (winter to winter), a transition is made from night
through full day to night again. Bishop Baldwin and the on-stage
Choir of Clerics will sing Latin motets throughout. The Off-stage
Choir also sings its designated pieces inter alia throughout.*

Moment by moment, sunrise by sunise,
season by season, and so the world turns.

NIGHT

MORGAN, LADY DE HAUTDESERT

Midwinter snowlight...Moment by moment
we overhaul yesterday. So the world turns.

WINTER

After the feast's glad hand,
the closed fist of Lent;
Christians atone for greed and pride
and set red meat aside.

The sun is fully up and the washing of Gawain *begins.*
The cuirass is brought forward.

DAY

BALDWIN, YWAIN, AGRAVAIN, THE FOOL

Here is your second flesh, your ribs of steel.
Which is the false flesh, which the real?

BALDWIN

Mors stupebit, et natura,
Cum resurget creatura
Judicanti responsura.

GAWAIN

I dreamed my enemy
standing before me; his sword
struck the shield; the blow
was weightless, soundless.

36

GUINEVERE

Here is the Golden Boy,
in love with his journey.
He dreams himself
taking the first few steps.

MORGAN, LADY DE HAUTDESERT

Wolves leave the bleak high ground   NIGHT
starved, impenitent;
unconsoled by sober faith
they howl in the wind's teeth.

The world is a treasury piled high with yesterdays: S
cash in our pockets. So the world turns.   P
                                                        R
                                                        I
Then comes the Lenten flower,   N
the first sudden thaw;   G
the long dark dreams of winter break
and hibernators wake.

The hauberk is brought forward.   DAY

BALDWIN, YWAIN, AGRAVAIN, THE FOOL

Here is the your second skin, your steel shawl.
Which is the live skin, which the caul?

BALDWIN

Rex tremendæ majestatis,
Qui salvandos salvas gratis,
Salva me, fons pietatis.

GAWAIN

I dreamed my enemy
standing before me; sunlight

poured on the shield; his eyes
glossed like the eyes of the blind.

Here is the court's darling,
dazzled by distances.
He dreams the adventure
advancing as he advances.

MORGAN, LADY DE HAUTDESERT

The fledgling's half-mad power –   NIGHT
shriek and open maw –
the bulge of sap in the purple bud,
the spring's hot blood –

Yesterday makes us remember tomorrow   S
– soon to be history. So the world turns.   U
                                                    M
                                                    M
– all mellows to fat, green leaf,   E
midsummer's midday hush,   R
broad wings on the valley floor,
a heat-haze on the moor.

The morion is brought forward.   DAY

BALDWIN, YWAIN, AGRAVAIN, THE FOOL

Here is your second skull, your cap of steel.
If both are sundered, which will heal?

BALDWIN

Juste judex ultionis,
Donum fac remissionis,
Ante diem rationis.

38

GAWAIN

I dreamed my enemy
standing before me; he stared
at the emblem, his gaze
fixed like someone watching water.

GUINEVERE

Here is the warrior, charmed
by his own recklessness.
He dreams the woodlands
cordoned by shadow.

MORGAN, LADY DE HAUTDESERT

The grain is green as belief,   NIGHT
meadows are heaped in their plush;
before the day has really begun
the sea is reined-in by the sun.

Tomorrow will stumble on yesterday's promises,   A
cancelling everything. So the world turns.   U
                                                  T
                                                  U
Next, the year's slow death;   M
a faint, dull blush   N
of decay in the bloom on fallen fruit;
mulch to feed the root.

The sword is brought forward.   DAY

BALDWIN, YWAIN, AGRAVAIN, THE FOOL

Here is your second arm, your steel sinew.
Which is the strong arm, which the true?

BALDWIN

Confutatis maledictis,
Flammis acribus addictis,
Voca me cum benedictis.

GAWAIN

I dreamed my enemy
standing close, his face
wiped clean; one finger traced
the knot's unbroken line.

GUINEVERE

Here is the only hero,
foxed by his own courage.
He dreams the fenlands
mobbed by mists.

MORGAN, LADY DE HAUTDESERT

Now comes the first full drench;   NIGHT
the world's half-loose
on its moorings in a piling gale
and the fields set sail.

The days are impatient; each hurries to be   W
tomorrow or yesterday. So the world turns.   I
                                                    N
                                                    T
Slowly the winter's winch   E
hauls sheets of ice   R
inland, and the ice-winds sing
the end of everything.

The shield is brought forward.   DAY

40

ARTHUR, YWAIN, AGRAVAIN, THE FOOL

Here is your badge of steel, the endless knot –
Weave your purpose into that.

Here is Solomon's sign – the emblem asks
fivefold virtues, fivefold tasks.

BALDWIN

Huic ergo parce, Deus.
Pie Jesu Domine,
Dona eis requiem.

GAWAIN

I dreamed my enemy
kneeling before me, his hands
raised like a supplicant's;
I gave him food and drink.

GUINEVERE

Here is the Golden Boy,
in love with his journey.
He dreams himself
taking the last few steps.

MORGAN, LADY DE HAUTDESERT

Gawain, can you smell that stench? –
the earth's a charnel house;
these are your journey's milestones:
the season's bare bones.

Moment by moment, we overhaul yesterday.
Midwinter snowlight...And so the world turns.

GAWAIN

All Soul's Day. The moment
waited for me.
I'm full of my journey
as a bird is full of flight.

MORGAN

Now with a single step –

THE FOOL

Look out of your window;
you might see
a shadow flowing over the stones in the courtyard.

Who is it?

MORGAN

Now, with a single step –

THE FOOL

Look out of your door;
you might see
someone closing another door in the hallway.

Who is it?

MORGAN

Now, with a single step –

THE FOOL

Look over the moor;
you might see

42

a rider coming towards you who gets no closer.

Who is it?

MORGAN

Now, with a single step –

THE FOOL

Look in your mirror;
you might see
the image of someone retreating before your face.

MORGAN

Now, with a single step, your journey starts.

THE FOOL

Who is it?

End of Act One

Act Two

Gawain about to embark on his journey. Morgan *has him in thrall.*
As before, we will see the travelling Knight who is, in effect, Gawain,
as he makes the journey described by Morgan.

MORGAN

Now, with a single step, your journey starts.

Through woods and over hills,
no food, no friend, no shelter... Into Wales,
past Holy Head, across into the Wirral -
a wilderness where murderers and thieves
guard every road and ford.

A single step, a mile, ten miles...

GAWAIN

Cross of Christ, save me.

MORGAN

The forest is broken markers, rags of maps;
wild things roam the place,
they have your scent; madmen watch from caves -
they seem to know, before you know yourself,

which way you'll choose to go.
Each one must be faced and each one killed.

A day, another day, a week of days...

GAWAIN

Cross of Christ, save me.

MORGAN

Winter closes in. The rivers run
straight from the snowline.
Night after night, near dead from the sleet,
you must sleep in your irons,
wedged between naked rocks.

Another mile, another day, another week...

GAWAIN

Cross of Christ, save me.

MORGAN

By day you go through bleak and frozen marshland,
hoar-frost thick as moss, ice over stone,
roosting birds too swollen with cold to sing...

GAWAIN

Cross of Christ, save me.

MORGAN

Mile after mile, day after day, week after week,
until your journey ends.

GAWAIN

Cross of Christ, save me.

The following lines, from Gawain, Morgan, Bertilak *and* Lady de Hautdesert, *are interjected during the course of the journey. As the journey is made, we will become aware of* Bertilak *and* Lady de Hautdesert *occupying the 'world inside' set as they await* Gawain's *arrival. The two areas (world inside/world outside) should be in part distinguished by the presence of two doors, standing flat to the auditorium. These represent either side of the same door. At the moment when the 'other'* Gawain *ends his journey, he should be confronting one of the doors (i.e. the outer side) by facing upstage. On the downstage side of the other door are* Lady de Hautdesert *and* Bertilak.

MORGAN

Now, with a single step, your journey starts.

GAWAIN

Cross of Christ, save me.

LADY DE HAUTDESERT

Soon...what you most love –

BERTILAK

– and what you fear.

MORGAN

A single step, a mile, ten miles.

GAWAIN

Cross of Christ, save me.

LADY DE HAUTDESERT

Soon...what you want, you'll have –

BERTILAK

                               – it's almost here.

MORGAN

A day, another day, a week of days.

GAWAIN

Cross of Christ, save me.

LADY DE HAUTDESERT

Soon you'll see it's face –

BERTILAK

                  – soon you'll hear its voice.

MORGAN

Another mile, another day, another week.

GAWAIN

Cross of Christ, save me.

LADY DE HAUTDESERT, BERTILAK

This is the hour of vanity or choice.

MORGAN

Mile after mile, day after day, week after week,
and now your journey ends,
this Christmas eve, and brings you...here.

47

The 'other' Gawain who has made the journey, is facing the door.

MORGAN

Night after night, the same dream:
my enemies under my hand, the old wounds opening.

The 'other' Gawain knocks at the door.

BERTILAK

Morgan...Your purpose chills me and excites me:
the bonds of treachery and kinship.

The 'other' Gawain knocks at the door again.

LADY DE HAUTDESERT

The promise is renewed
now, at the year's dead end.

*The 'other' Gawain knocks a third time at the door. Both doors open.
The 'other' Gawain walks through his door, as the 'true' Gawain
steps through to join* Lady de Hautdesert *and* Bertilak. *The doors
close and the 'other' Gawain exits unseen.* Bertilak *and* Lady de
Hautdesert *get up, smiling. In the following passage,* Morgan's
*interjections are akin to 'prompts', apart from her comment 'So close',
where she is gloating over* Gawain's *imminent dilemma.*

BERTILAK

Welcome...welcome...welcome...
Do you want food? Here's food.
This wine is my best.

LADY DE HAUTDESERT

Will you sit with us?

MORGAN

Here's your place...

LADY DE HAUTDESERT

Here's your place.

Gawain *sits with them, though he hesitates at first.*

BERTILAK

Tell me about your journey. Have you come far?
Tell me about the dangers that you met.
Where have you come from?

MORGAN

Tell your name...

BERTILAK

Will you tell your name?

GAWAIN

I've come from Arthur's court. My name's Gawain.

BERTILAK

Gawain.

LADY DE HAUTDESERT

Gawain.

BERTILAK

Now we shall learn
something of courtly love.

LADY DE HAUTDESERT

Now we shall learn... Everyone knows
of Gawain's skill in the art of love:
his gentleness, his honour, his soft speech.
You must be our teacher –

MORGAN

Help us to learn...

LADY DE HAUTDESERT

Help us to learn
the proper pace of passion;
help us to learn
the distance between objection and desire;
help us to learn
how to take love's scent,
how to draw the quarry, how to guess
its line of flight; help us to learn
how to run it down and then -
bring it to hand.

MORGAN

This house is yours...

BERTILAK

This house is yours, and everything
within this house is yours while you are here.
My food, my wine, my hearth,
good company, good conversation, sport,
everything...whatever you might want...

Take it; it's yours...

BERTILAK

Take it; it's yours. Stay with us here
this Christmas tide
and prosper from our company, and God's.

GAWAIN

My journey was hard: some enemy
at every turn, as in a dream...

LADY DE HAUTDESERT

Your journey is over.

GAWAIN

Or else it's just begun...
I have a debt to pay. My life is staked
on a promise; I cannot rest
here or anywhere
until I've found the Green Chapel
and the knight who holds that ground.
My dreams of death
have journeyed with me –
the bargain's struck, I carry it
closer than my shadow.

Bertilak *laughs – delighted, it seems, to be able to solve* Gawain's
problem.

BERTILAK

Sleep long, rise late, rest here
until you choose to leave;

The Green Chapel's nearby –
two miles, perhaps, no more.

MORGAN

So close...

GAWAIN

So close...The moment
of vanity and loss;
the choice of no choice...

BERTILAK

Stay in your room tomorrow
until the hour for mass.
Eat when you please; the household
will keep your time; my wife
will keep you company.

Bertilak's *last remark causes him difficulty; he tries to say it lightly,
but apprehensiveness betrays him.* Gawain *detects some of this. He
looks first at* Bertilak, *then at* Lady de Hautdesert, *whose eyes are
on her husband.* Morgan *is also looking at* Bertilak. *She seems angry,
as if she suspected he might be about to displease her.* Bertilak *has just
thought of a ploy and is eager to establish it.*

BERTILAK

I shall spend my days
hunting – dawn to dusk.
Let's make a pact
to exchange our trophies.
Each night, when I return,
whatever I've culled
I must give to you;

whatever you might have gained
you must give to me.

Lady de Hautdesert *is amused by her husband's jealousy and by the
implications of the pact. Clearly, it's a device to keep her faithful.*
Morgan *is furious.*

GAWAIN

Gain? What could I gain?

Bertilak *shrugs.*

GAWAIN

And how can I lose –
since whatever falls to me
must first be yours?

BERTILAK

Then gamble it.

Bertilak *lifts his glass, indicating to* Gawain *that he should do the
same.*

BERTILAK

Good fortune or bad -
let's drink to it.

They drink. Lady de Hautdesert *gets up and holds out a hand to*
Gawain.*She then leads him towards an area of the stage which serves
as* Gawain's *bedroom. A bed is there. Their movements, as they go
towards the bed, are a kind of emotional pavane: she is flirtatious,
while he avoids her advances. Their movements might parody the
forthcoming hunt scenes.* Lady de Hautdesert *leaves* Gawain *by the
bed and returns.* Bertilak *is watching her anxiously. As she nears*

him, he moves, in relation to her, much as she moved in relation to
Gawain; *she, for her part, moves as* Gawain *moved, avoiding her*
husband's attempts to confront her. They exit. Morgan *crosses to*
Gawain, *who is lying on the bed.*

MORGAN

Lie down without fear of the dark

> – lulla –

Sleep without fear of the dream

> – lulla –

Wake without fear of the day

> – lulla, lullaby...

During the lullaby, we see an image from a nightmare, as if Gawain
were dreaming it. The image should be drawn from what has gone
before: The Green Knight's *head being severed, perhaps, or the axe*
being lofted.

GAWAIN

Cross of Christ...

Morgan *moves upstage as* Lady de Hautdesert *crosses to the bed.*
Bertilak *(in the world outside) begins to hunt a stag. The hunt and*
the attempted seduction of Gawain *by* Lady de Hautdesert *will*
interweave. Gawain *wakes. The stag starts up.*

LADY DE HAUTDESERT

The door was unlocked.
If I were your enemy,
how simple to take you prisoner.

Are you my enemy?
Should I sue for terms?

The hunt: *the stag is flushed from cover.*

LADY DE HAUTDESERT

No terms, and no parole.
You are Gawain; the world adores you.
No ransom could buy me off.

The household is asleep.
My husband went out at dawn
with huntsmen and dogs. No one is here.

My body is yours.
Does it please you?
Do what you like with it.

The hunt: *the stag appears cornered.* Gawain *seems not to have registered her last remark.*

GAWAIN

Does the world adore me?
Is it true?

I'm not that hero.
No one has ever said so, except you.

LADY DE HAUTDESERT

If I were all women, all loveliness,
all wealth, all power –
then I'd be your match.

GAWAIN

Is that my price?
No one could own so much...
except, perhaps, your husband –
who owns *you*.

The hunt: the stag is in flight.

LADY DE HAUTDESERT

You *seem* to be Gawain –
prove that you are.
Prove your breeding, prove
that you've learned romance by rote,
and kiss me – as you should – before I go.

Lady de Hautdesert *kisses* Gawain.

The hunt : Bertilak *has cornered the stag. He kills it.* Lady de
Hautdesert *exits.* Morgan *moves downstage. As before, her presence,
her words, seem to leave* Gawain *tranced.*

MORGAN

A gift he must not refuse
but can't accept.
It is an empty mirror;
it is giving without loss.

We hear three knocks. Gawain *emerges from the trance.*

GAWAIN

Who's there...?

Now the game begins:
you must give what you've gained.

Bertilak *crosses to confront* Gawain. *In one hand he is carrying offal
cut from the stag, in the other, the stag's head. He throws the offal
back into the world outside set; the head he throws at* Gawain's *feet.*

BERTILAK

That's the raven's fee...
And this is yours.
Does it please you?
Do what you like with it.
Remember our bargain –
your winnings belong to me.

Gawain *kisses* Bertilak.

BERTILAK

That was your trophy?

GAWAIN

No – yours.

BERTILAK

Where did you find such pickings?

GAWAIN

Our contract didn't allow
for question and answer.
I've paid my debt.

BERTILAK

Tomorrow, I'll hunt again.
The bargain stands,
an exchange of winnings –

GAWAIN

– my trophy for yours –

BERTILAK

– no matter how rare –

GAWAIN

– no matter who profits most –

BERTILAK

– whatever the prey,
whatever the gain or loss.

Morgan *begins her lullaby as she crosses to the bed. When she reaches it,* Gawain *is sleeping.*

MORGAN

Lie down without fear of the dark

                    – lulla –

Sleep without fear of the dream

                    – lulla –

Wake without fear of the day

                    – lulla, lullaby...

As before, we see the moment from the nightmare.

GAWAIN

Cross of Christ...

Lady de Hautdesert *enters as the lullaby ends*. Morgan *goes upstage as* Lady de Hautdesert *crosses to the bed. In the world outside set*, Bertilak *begins to hunt a boar*. Gawain *wakes*.

LADY DE HAUTDESERT

Are you Gawain?
Surely you know love's rules...
Yesterday I took a kiss from you;
it's your turn now
to take from me whatever pleases you.

· GAWAIN

You didn't take the kiss:
you gave it...

The hunt: *the boar breaks through and runs past Bertilak.*

LADY DE HAUTDESERT

Did I break the rules? Then so can you -
you're strong, I'm here alone;
my rashness is your excuse
for whatever you choose to do.

GAWAIN

Unless my choice
is: say nothing, do nothing.

Lady de Hautdesert *kisses* Gawain.

The hunt: Bertilak *circles, intercepting the boar's line of retreat.*

LADY DE HAUTDESERT

You're skilled in love.

I'm too dull
to learn the craft, too careless.

GAWAIN

Or else too passionate.

Lady de Hautdesert *kisses* Gawain.

The hunt: *the boar is killed by* Bertilak. Lady de Hautdesert *exits.*
Morgan *moves downstage; as before, her words fix* Gawain.

MORGAN

A word he must not hear
but can't ignore.
It is a blind light;
it is speech without pity.

We hear three knocks. Gawain *comes-to, as before.*

GAWAIN

Who's there...?

MORGAN

Now you must trade
token for token: a game where no one wins.

Bertilak *crosses to confront* Gawain. *He is carrying the boar's head.*
He throws this down in front of Gawain.

BERTILAK

Here's your trophy.

GAWAIN

And here is yours.

Gawain *kisses* Bertilak *twice*.

GAWAIN

It's all I have.

BERTILAK

All... I wish I had as much.

GAWAIN

You have – that was our bargain.
Nothing I win
goes with me when I leave.
You own it now.

BERTILAK

Tomorrow, the same exchange –

GAWAIN

– whatever I gain is yours –

BERTILAK

– no matter what it is,
no matter what the cost.

Morgan *begins her lullaby as she crosses to the bed. When she reaches it*, Gawain *is sleeping*.

MORGAN

Lie down without fear of the dark
                           – lulla –
Sleep without fear of the dream
                           – lulla –

Wake without fear of the day

                              – lulla, lullaby...

As before: the nightmare moment.

GAWAIN

Cross of Christ...

Lady de Hautdesert *enters as the lullaby ends. She is wearing a skimpy gown, bound at the waist with a green sash.* Morgan *goes upstage as* Lady de Hautdesert *crosses to the bed and lies down on it next to* Gawain. *In the world outside set,* Bertilak *begins to hunt a fox.* Gawain *wakes.* (Lady de Hautdesert *is now in love with* Gawain).

LADY DE HAUTDESERT

Winter sun on melting snow: it's blinding...
I lay here while you slept;
it seemed your head
burned with a dark flame.
It blurred my eye.

Lady de Hautdesert *kisses* Gawain.

The hunt: *the fox runs in one direction and is cut off.*

LADY DE HAUTDESERT

How could you sleep?
I seemed to hear your voice... All night
it beat against my brow.
I couldn't breathe.
I listened to the ice-wind, and your voice.

Lady de Hautdesert *kisses* Gawain.

The hunt: *the fox runs in another direction and is cut off.*

LADY DE HAUTDESERT

The future stares me down.
I'm twinned with another woman –dingy, wild,
deadlocked by knowledge.
Why won't you have my love?

Lady de Hautdesert *kisses* Gawain.

The hunt: *the fox takes a third direction and is cut off.*

Lady de Hautdesert *removes her sash and offers it to* Gawain, *who won't take it.*

GAWAIN

Your love, your grief, your favour –
you own these things, not me.

LADY DE HAUTDESERT

That's the hardest lesson...
But take this –
while you wear it, nothing can hurt you.

Gawain *takes the sash and looks at it.*

GAWAIN

Nothing?

LADY DE HAUTDESERT

Axe-stroke, sword-stroke, lance;
if you wear this, you cannot die.

Gawain *wraps the sash round his waist.* Morgan *has entered. We see that she is tense with glee when* Gawain *puts on the sash.*

63

The hunt: Bertilak *kills the fox.* Lady de Hautdesert *withdraws towards* Morgan *whose words, as before, fix* Gawain.

MORGAN

A choice he has to face
but cannot make.
It is a shut fist;
it is the choice of no choice.

We hear three knocks. Gawain *comes-to.*

GAWAIN

Who's there...?

MORGAN

Now the game ends
and I gain everything.

Bertilak *crosses to confront* Gawain. Gawain *kisses* Bertilak *three times.*

BERTILAK

I hunted all day,
but all I took was this –

Bertilak *throws down the carcass of the fox.*

BERTILAK

– a poor exchange:
vermin for three clean kisses.

Bertilak *puts his fingertips to his lips.*

BERTILAK

And that was all – three kisses?

GAWAIN

All.

BERTILAK

I hope you got them cheaply.
Three kisses...

GAWAIN

That was all.
    Now my time here is over.

BERTILAK

Now my task here is over;
a new task begins.
In another place,
we'll play another game.

MORGAN, LADY DE HAUTDESERT

Soon – the moment that waited for you
as you journeyed towards it...

GAWAIN

Fear of death
like a dark flame...

MORGAN, LADY DE HAUTDESERT

Soon – the moment you carried with you
from the worst dream...

GAWAIN

Fear of death
like an ice-wind...

MORGAN, LADY DE HAUTDESERT

The contract can't be broken;
it's your burden...

GAWAIN

Fear of death
like a voice beating my brow...

Now my time here is over.

LADY DE HAUTDESERT

One life here is over,
another begins.
Everything's changed
except my face and name.

Lady de Hautdesert *exits.*

Gawain *now undertakes his journey to the Green Chapel. As before,*
Morgan *has him in thrall.*

MORGAN

Now you set foot on the threshold,
the world outdoors
before you, like a map of dreams.

Now you set foot on the ground,
the world indoors
behind you, like forgotten promises.

There is the road – the Green Chapel
almost in sight. Now you must choose.
Turn back. No one will know.
Turn back. Save your life. No one will know.

We see the 'other Gawain' crossing a landscape. Morgan *retreats,
but stays on stage. We hear* The Green Knight's *voice, coming closer
until he finally steps into view carrying the axe.*

THE GREEN KNIGHT

(Off)

Gawain!

GAWAIN

Fear of death
like a dark flame...

THE GREEN KNIGHT

(Off)

Gawain!

GAWAIN

Fear of death
like an ice-wind...

THE GREEN KNIGHT

(Comes into view)

Gawain!

Fear of death
like a voice beating my brow.

The Green Knight *approaches* Gawain.

THE GREEN KNIGHT

A year and a day
since you made your promise;
a year and a day
since you swung the axe;

since you saw my head
lopped and fallen –

GAWAIN

– your eyes clouded with blood,
your mouth filling with blood –

THE GREEN KNIGHT

– now see your own face there,
your eyes, your mouth, your blood.

GAWAIN

My eyes, my mouth, my blood.

THE GREEN KNIGHT

Now I shall see
your body polled and pruned
like any tree.

Gawain *steps forward to receive the axe-blow.*

GAWAIN

Now I acquit myself:
a blow for a blow, a debt, a death.

MORGAN

Night after night, the same dream –
my enemies under my hand,
the old wounds opening.

Gawain *bows his head.* The Green Knight *swings the axe.* Gawain *ducks back, avoiding the blow.*

THE GREEN KNIGHT

Are you Gawain?
You flinch from the axe.
Remember the rules we made
when I stood in Arthur's court
and bowed my head to you.

MORGAN

Here is my contract – burden for burden...

Gawain *steps forward and bows his head once more.* The Green Knight *swings the axe, but stops short of delivering the blow.* Gawain *hasn't flinched.*

THE GREEN KNIGHT

You are Gawain.
Pride and courage
kept you on your mark.

Gawain *doesn't understand why* The Green Knight *should have delayed the blow, unless he's simply prolonging the moment in order to be cruel. He lifts his head and looks at* The Green Knight.

69

GAWAIN

I'n not that hero.
No one ever said so.

Gawain *bows his head again.*

GAWAIN

My life is light – easier to lift
than the axe. I remember our pledge.
Now – take your turn.

MORGAN

...loss for loss, sorrow for sorrow,
and terrible freedoms, freely given.

The Green Knight *swings the axe, grazing* Gawain's *neck and
fetching blood from a superficial wound.* Gawain *can't understand
why he's been spared.*

GAWAIN

Why taunt me with a token death?
I stood my ground.
Kill me, or let me go.

THE GREEN KNIGHT

The first blow was a feint;
the second, too.
Twice you were honest –
the kisses you got each day
you traded fairly;
but when you were given the sash
you lied to keep it.

70

I cut you for that untruth,
but didn't kill you;
it wasn't greed or love that made you lie,
but fear of death –
not sin enough to die for.

Gawain *strips off the sash and holds it out to the* Green Knight.

GAWAIN

Not greed and love?
I'm guilty of both.
I wanted fame. I loved myself too much.
I'm guilty of cowardice, too.
Take this. I can't be shriven
while I possess it.

The Green Knight *loops the sash across* Gawain's *chest.*

THE GREEN KNIGHT

It's yours; you carry it
closer than your shadow.

Now you must go back,
over the winter badlands,
your shoulders hoisted to the ice-wind.

Dreams of death
will journey with you
like something you've hoarded,
like something you need to own.

Go back, take what you've earned;
Go back, take what you've learned.
Go back...

MORGAN

Your purpose has ended; become yourself.

The Green Knight *exits*

GAWAIN

Cross of Christ, save me...

THE GREEN KNIGHT

(Off)

Go back...

GAWAIN

Cross of Christ!

THE GREEN KNIGHT

(Off)

Go back...

Morgan's *magic shape-shifts* The Green Knight *who is revealed as* Bertilak. Gawain *sees this and reacts.*

MORGAN

My power shape-shifted him
from man to hero – from hero back to man.
I've done the same to you.
Become yourself; your purpose has just begun.
Now you must go back,
taking with you everything you've gained:
greed, self-love and cowardice.
Now you must go back; your journey starts....

During Gawain's *journey back, the court re-appears on stage –*
Arthur, Guinevere, Agravain, Ywain, Baldwin, The Fool.
Gawain *will enter as did* The Green Knight *in Act One.*

GUINEVERE

Arthur – join us.
Come and sit by me.

ARTHUR

Who's brave?
Who'll prove his courage to me?

THE FOOL

Something stranger than charity,
something greener than grief;
something colder than justice,
more secret, more stern than belief.

What is it?

We hear a knock at the door.

ARTHUR

Who's brave?

We hear a knock at the door.

GUINEVERE

Come and take your place.

A knock at the door – The Fool *opens it.* Morgan *enters . She is
invisible to the court.*

73

MORGAN

Soon you'll see its face,
soon you'll hear its voice.

ARTHUR

It's nothing...nothing...nothing...
A game, an escapade,
Christmas mummery, a raree show...

Can't someone whet
my appetite with courage?

THE FOOL

My first two make a man,
my third makes me a woman;
add nothing and the world adores me.

Who is it?

We hear a knock at the door.

MORGAN

Here is a face
shrouded by the weather.

We hear a knock at the door.

MORGAN

Here is a voice
baffled by endless echoes.

We hear a knock at the door. The door opens. Gawain *enters. His features and outer-garments are thick with snow. The members of the court stare at him as if he were an apparition. Then, as he strikes snow*

74

from his face and coat, they see who it is and crowd round him, excited and eager. They help him remove his greatcoat.

MEMBERS OF THE COURT

Gawain...Gawain...Gawain...

ARTHUR

Welcome...welcome...welcome....

YWAIN

Tell us of wolves and worms.

AGRAVAIN

Tell us of furies and fiends.

THE FOOL

Tell us of raw-head and bloody-bones.

YWAIN

Tell us how you ran to battle,

BALDWIN

how you called on Christ,

AGRAVAIN

how your sword smoked...

MEMBERS OF THE COURT

Tell all, all as it was...

GAWAIN

I'm not that hero.

(*to* Arthur)

Are you still king?

MEMBERS OF THE COURT

(*Variously*)

God's name...
You dare...

ARTHUR

Are you tired?

GUINEVERE

Then rest.

ARTHUR

Are you harrowed?

GUINEVERE

Here's your calm.

ARTHUR

Are you hurt?

GUINEVERE

Here's your cure.

ARTHUR

Unarm, and sit with us –

GUINEVERE

– here's your place.

ARTHUR

All as it was, nothing changed.

MORGAN

All as it was...except for dreams
of fear and fame, except for lies,
except for the sash, token of loss,
except for broken promises,
except for the cost of cowardice,
except for this man with dirty hands.

ARTHUR

Piece by piece, let go your armour,

GUINEVERE

let go hardship,

THE FOOL

let go the world outside.

BALDWIN

Piece by piece, tell us everything –

YWAIN

spice our food with news of victories

AGRAVAIN

and colours brought home in glory.

MEMBERS OF THE COURT

All as it was...

One by one, the members of the court step forward and disarm
Gawain, *each removing a piece of armour. They ask him, again, to*
satisfy them about his courage and his adventures. His responses
anger and disappoint them. One by one, they move away, each taking
his (or her) place in a tableau that echoes their positions at the
beginning of Act One.

Baldwin *removes the cuirass.*

BALDWIN

Here is your second flesh, your ribs of steel.

Tell me of victories –
how you trusted in Christ's five wounds.

MEMBERS OF THE COURT

All as it was...

GAWAIN

Moment by moment, we overhaul yesterday;
secrets and sorrow...so the world turns.

BALDWIN

(Angrily)

Tell me of victories!

MEMBERS OF THE COURT

All as it was...

MORGAN

Except for dreams of fear and fame.

GAWAIN

Who do you want me to be?
I'm not that hero.

BALDWIN

When you are more yourself,
I'll ask again.

Baldwin *moves away and take his place.* Agravain *removes the hauberk.*

AGRAVAIN

Here is your second skin, your steel shawl.

Tell me of honour –
how you trusted the Virgin's five joys.

MEMBERS OF THE COURT

All as it was...

GAWAIN

The world is a treasury – cash in our pockets,
stolen or squandered...so the world turns.

AGRAVAIN

(Angrily)

Tell me of honour!

MEMBERS OF THE COURT

All as it was...

MORGAN

Except for lies, except for the sash.

GAWAIN

Why do you ask?
Who do you want me to be?
I'm not that hero.

AGRAVAIN

When you are more yourself,
we'll speak again.

Agravain *moves away and takes his place.* Ywain *removes the morion.*

YWAIN

Here is your second skull, your cap of steel.

Tell me of courage –
How you trusted in your five senses.

MEMBERS OF THE COURT

All as it was...

GAWAIN

Yesterday makes us remember tomorrow,
better forgotten...so the world turns.

YWAIN

(Angrily)

Tell me of courage!

MEMBERS OF THE COURT

All as it was...

MORGAN

Except for broken promises.

GAWAIN

Why do you ask
for someone who isn't here?
Who do you want me to be?
I'm not that hero.

YWAIN

When you are more yourself,
tell me again.

Ywain *moves away and takes his place.* Arthur *takes the sword.*

ARTHUR

Prove your courage to me.
Tell how you made your five fingers
one fist, so no one could break your hold.

MEMBERS OF THE COURT

All as it was...

ARTHUR

You made the journey
through mists and swarming shadows,
waiting for the worst dream to begin.
Now here you stand,
delivered from the dream,
glorious with wounds and trophies.

MEMBERS OF THE COURT

All as it was...

MORGAN

Except for the cost of cowardice.

GAWAIN

Tomorrow will stumble on yesterday's promises,
each of them broken...so the world turns.

ARTHUR

(Angrily)

Prove your courage to me!

MEMBERS OF THE COURT

All as it was...

GAWAIN

What do you want to see –
a mirror-image retreating before your face?
Someone who isn't here?
Who do you want me to be?
I'm not that hero.

ARTHUR

When you are more yourself,
speak to me then.

Arthur *moves away and takes his place.* Guinevere *removes the sash from around* Gawain's *body.*

They were singing your courage
before you were out of sight.
Your legend was born
before your memory was old –'Gawain'
on every lip, as if
you'd left your name behind.

MEMBERS OF THE COURT

All as it was...

MORGAN

Except for this man with dirty hands.

GAWAIN

Moment by moment, we overhaul yesterday;
falsehood and vanity...so the world turns.

GUINEVERE

They were singing your courage...

GAWAIN

No one can be your joy
or your disgrace; the mirror
gives you no one's face
except your own; don't ask
for the person you want me to be;
I'm not that hero.

GUINEVERE

Now you are more yourself,
let's speak again.

Guinevere *moves away and takes her place.*

THE FOOL

All as it was, all completely changed...

MEMBERS OF THE COURT

All as it was, all completely changed...

THE FOOL

All as it was, all completely changed,
like a name grown unfamiliar,
like a man returned from a journey
with nothing familiar about him
except his name.

The Fool *moves away and takes his place.*

MEMBERS OF THE COURT

All as it was, all completely changed...

MORGAN

Night after night, the same dream,
my enemies under my hand,
the old wounds opening...

GAWAIN

I left this place
full of my journey, as a bird
is full of flight.

Everyone here
lived from golden
moment to golden moment;

84

we expected nothing
but innocence, nothing
but constancy, nothing

that would tarnish
or grow old, nothing
but perfect love.

Now I'm home again,
sullen, empty-handed, feverish
with knowledge.

How will I live
in this tyranny of virtue?
I am the sudden guest,

unwanted, raw
as winter weather, bringing news
no one hoped to hear.

I'm a spoiled reputation,
I'm bad blood,
a symptom of sorrow...

They looked for someone glorious
with wounds and trophies.
I'm not that hero.

MORGAN

Now, at the year's dead end
the same promise
of terrible freedoms, freely given.

Look out of your window;
you might see
a shadow flowing over the stones in the courtyard.

Look in your mirror;
you might see
the image of someone retreating before your face.

Think only of dreams and promises.

Then

        with a single step

                your journey starts.

The door opens and Morgan *exits into the world outside.*

END

Appendix

Bishop Baldwin's solo passages during the arming of Gawain
are taken from the *Dies Irae*. It was customary, on All Soul's
Day, that three masses should be offered for the souls of the
faithful dead and that the *Dies Irae* should be sung.

The texts of the Marian antiphons sung by Bishop Baldwin and
the on-stage Choir of Clerics during the arming of Gawain are
as follows:

1. Alma Redemptoris Mater, quæ pervia cæli Porta manes,
   Et stella maris, succurre cadenti Surgere qui curat populo:
   Tu quæ genuisti, Natura mirante, tuum sanctum Genitorem:
   Virgo prius ac posterius, Gabrielis ab ore Sumens illud Ave,
   peccatorum miserere.

2. Ave Regina cælorum,
   Ave Domina Angelorum:
   Salve radix, salve porta,
   Ex qua mundo lux est orta:
   Gaude Virgo gloriosa,
   Super omnes speciosa:
   Vale O valde decora,
   Et pro nobis Christum exora.

3. Regina cæli lætare, alleluia:
    Quia quem meruisti portare, alleluia:
    Resurrexit, sicut dixit, alleluia:
    Ora pro nobis Deum, alleluia.

4. Salve, Regina, mater misercordiae:
    Vita, dulcedo, et spes nostra, salve.
    Ad te clamamus, exsules, filii Hevae.
    Ad te suspiramus, gementes et flentes in hac lacrimarum
    valle.
    Eia ergo, Advocata nostra, illos tuos misericordes oculos
    ad nos converte.
    Et Jesum, benedictum fructum ventris tui, nobis post hoc
    exsilium ostende.
    O clemens: O pia: O dulcis Virgo Maria.

5. Here, the 'Alma Redemptoris Mater...' is repeated.